Scientists and their Discoveries

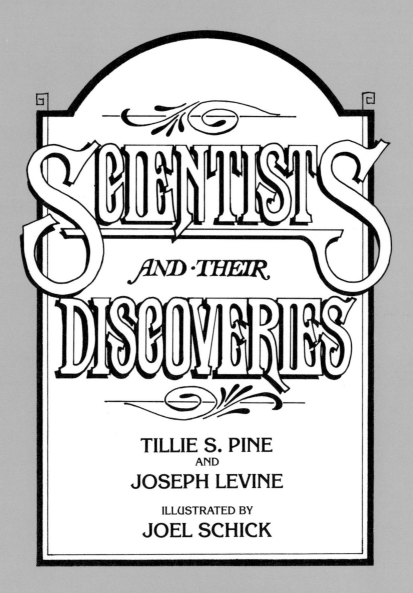

SCIENTISTS AND THEIR DISCOVERIES

TILLIE S. PINE
AND
JOSEPH LEVINE

ILLUSTRATED BY
JOEL SCHICK

MCGRAW-HILL BOOK COMPANY

NEW YORK ST. LOUIS SAN FRANCISCO AUCKLAND BOGOTÁ
DÜSSELDORF JOHANNESBURG LONDON MADRID MEXICO
MONTREAL NEW DELHI PANAMA PARIS SÃO PAULO SINGAPORE
SYDNEY TOKYO TORONTO

To Alan and Jennifer
and to Abby and Julie for making life a series
of creative activities and happy experiences

Library of Congress Cataloging in Publication Data

Pine, Tillie S.
Scientists and their discoveries.

SUMMARY: Explains in simple language the
discoveries and investigations of famous
scientists including Galileo, Benjamin Franklin,
Thomas Alva Edison, and Robert Goddard.
1. Scientists—Juvenile literature.
2. Science—History—Juvenile literature.
[1. Science—History. 2. Scientists]
I. Levine, Joseph, joint author. II. Schick,
Joel. III. Title.
Q141.P48   509′.2′2   [B]   77-26607
ISBN 0-07-050120-3

123456789   RABP   78321098

INTRODUCTION

Do you know
  why you weigh less in water than out of water,
  who found out that the Sun is the center of our Universe,
  who the first American scientist was,
  who the "father of modern rocketry" is,
  who discovered what the "man in the Moon" really is,
  why the Moon does not fly away from the Earth
                    and
  why the planets do not fly away from the Sun?

In this book you will find the answers to these questions
and to others. You will learn that the scientists and
inventors were real people. Usually they worked alone but
sometimes they worked with other scientists. Some of these
scientists made their discoveries long, long ago. Since
then, other scientists have used these discoveries to make
still other wonderful findings. You will realize that what
these scientists discovered affected the lives of people,
long ago and today.

  You will read about what you yourself can do to help
you understand what our great scientists found out.

Pythagoras (Sixth century B.C.)

Have you ever wondered why violinists and guitarists from time to time tighten or loosen the strings on their instruments?

Long ago a man who was named Pythagoras was born in ancient Greece, where he grew up. He was a brilliant student. Soon he became famous as an astronomer and as a great mathematician. Pythagoras was also interested in music. One day he was passing a blacksmith's shop, where a blacksmith was working. He became aware that when the blacksmith hit anvils of different sizes, they made different tones. Pythagoras wondered what caused the differences in the tones. He went home and experimented with sounds by stretching and then plucking strings of different lengths. He discovered that the longer the string, the lower the tone it made; the shorter the string, the higher the tone. This discovery helped him realize why the different anvils gave off different tones when they were struck. He concluded that the larger the anvil, the lower the tone, and the smaller the anvil, the higher the tone.

So—Pythagoras' curiosity about the sounds heard when anvils were struck led him to investigate the reason why the sounds of different vibrating strings were different.

When we make musical instruments of all kinds and sizes, we still use what Pythagoras discovered about tones. We make long-stringed instruments, like cellos, whose vibrating strings make low tones, and short-stringed instruments, like violins, that make higher tones. We can change the pitch of a string by changing the length of the vibrating part. We also make large wind instruments, like tubas, whose vibrating, long air columns make low tones, and small wind instruments, like flutes, whose vibrating shorter air columns make higher tones.

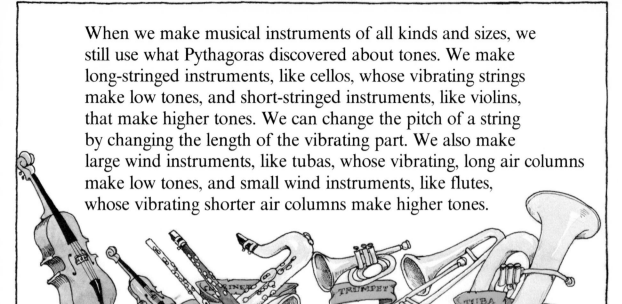

You can find out how to get different tones from a single vibrating string.
Place a strong rubberband around a covered box.
Raise the band at one end by placing a pencil under it.
Pluck the "string." Listen to the sound. Now—shorten the band's length by pressing the string against the box.
Pluck the band again. Does the tone change? Do you hear a higher or a lower tone? Keep shortening the band and plucking the "string." Do you see that the longer the vibrating string, the lower the tone, the shorter the string, the higher the tone?

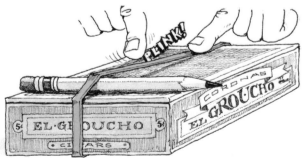

Experiment with tone changes using thin bands and thick bands, loose bands and tight bands. Which make lower tones and which make higher tones?

Archimedes (278 B.C.–212 B.C.)

Archimedes was a famous scientist and inventor. He lived in Greece more than 2,000 years ago. It was he who discovered that when an object is put into water, the water pushes up against it and makes the object weigh less. This pushing force is called *buoyancy*. One day, the story goes, Archimedes stepped into a tub full of water. Some of the water overflowed the tub. He realized that he took up space in the water.

He decided that he felt lighter because the water in the tub buoyed him up. He found out that the amount of water that overflowed weighed the same as the amount of weight his body "lost" in the water.

Archimedes also found out the reasons why things can float in water. He wrote books that explained his discoveries. Archimedes was outstanding in mathematics and engineering. He was also the first scientist to explain how a worker using a lever can lift very heavy weights. He said, "Give me a place to stand and a lever long enough and I will move the Earth."

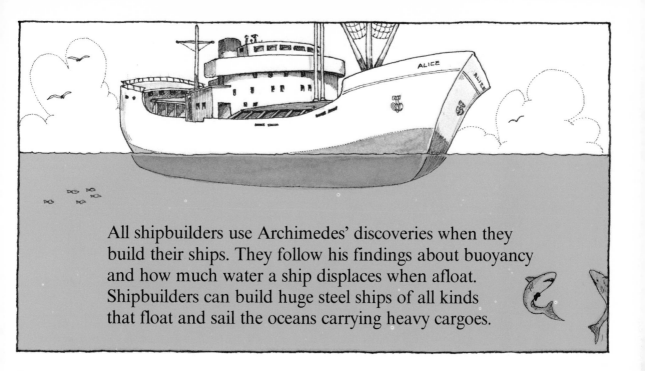

All shipbuilders use Archimedes' discoveries when they
build their ships. They follow his findings about buoyancy
and how much water a ship displaces when afloat.
Shipbuilders can build huge steel ships of all kinds
that float and sail the oceans carrying heavy cargoes.

You can prove that when an object is put into water it weighs
less than it does out of water. You need a small jar with
a cover, strong rubberbands, a paper clip, a ruler and a sink
full of water. Fill the jar with pebbles, sand or marbles
and cover it. Place one rubberband tightly around the neck
of the jar. Attach the clip to the rubberband. Attach the
other rubberband to the other end of the clip. Hold the
second rubberband and lift up the jar. What happens? Why?
Measure the length of the stretched rubberband. Now, lower
the jar into the water in the sink. Make sure that the jar
does not touch the bottom of the sink. What happens to the
stretched rubberband this time? Measure it again.
Why is the rubberband shorter?
Does this experiment show you what happens to the weight of
an object in water?

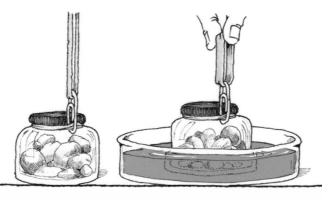

Nicolaus Copernicus (1473–1543)

For thousands of years before Copernicus was born in Poland
in 1473, people believed that the Earth was the center of the
Universe. They thought that all the heavenly bodies revolved
around it. Copernicus studied medicine, religion, mathematics
and science when he went to college. It was then that he
became very much interested in astronomy. He read all the
books he could find about it. After many years of observing
the sky, and measuring the heavenly bodies with a very simple
instrument called a cross-staff, he became convinced that
the Earth could *not* be the center of the Universe. Copernicus
decided that the Sun was the center of the Universe and that
the Earth was one of the planets that revolved around the Sun.
He also believed, as did some scientists long before his time,
that the Earth turned on its own axis, giving us day and night.
About one year before Copernicus died, at the age of seventy, his
book "About the Revolution of the Heavenly Bodies" was published.

Scientists know that Copernicus was right in believing that the Sun is the center of our Solar System. They use instruments such as telescopes and cameras to observe the heavenly bodies of our system. With these instruments, scientists are able to measure accurately the distances and the movements of the planets in their orbits around the Sun. Scientists are also using atomic clocks to measure time very, very accurately in their studies of space.

Visit a planetarium and see models, pictures and movies that show and tell you all about the Solar System. You will see how the nine planets revolve around the Sun. You will find out which ones are nearer to the Earth and which ones are farther away, and you will see how the planets differ in size. Draw pictures and diagrams of our Solar System showing the sizes and positions of the planets in their orbits around the Sun. Make a model of the Solar System using different-size balls and round fruits and vegetables to represent the nine planets and the Sun. Hang the "planets" from a wire clothes hanger showing their positions in "space" with the "Sun" in the center.

Galileo Galilei (1564–1642)

Galileo was born in Italy and during his long lifetime, he discovered many important laws of science. When he heard that a Dutch lens maker, Hans Lippershey, had made a toy using lenses through which he saw far-away things a little closer and larger, Galileo used this idea and soon made the first successful spyglass, or telescope. He put an inward curved (concave) lens into one end of a piece of pipe and an outward curved (convex) lens into the other end. When he looked through this telescope, he could see things three times larger than they appeared to his naked eye. After many experiments, he was able to make a telescope that helped him see things thirty-three times enlarged. Now he could observe ships far out at sea that he could not see without his telescope.
It was through his telescope that Galileo discovered that the "man in the Moon" was really mountains and plains on the moon's surface. He was the first scientist to see that the planet Jupiter had moons of its own.

Galileo was the first one to explain how a pendulum works, and this led to the making of pendulum clocks. He also discovered that things gain speed as they fall.
Galileo was a great mathematician and astronomer. He is said to be one of the greatest scientists the world has ever known.

Using Galileo's ideas, we make all kinds of instruments that use lenses to help us observe things much larger and much nearer. We make opera glasses, binoculars and field glasses. We make giant telescopes that use mirrors that measure about seventeen feet (a little more than five meters) across. Through them we see distant moons and planets and their moons close up. Through these telescopes we study distant stars. We also use lenses to make microscopes that help us observe very, very tiny plants and animals that cannot be seen with the naked eye.

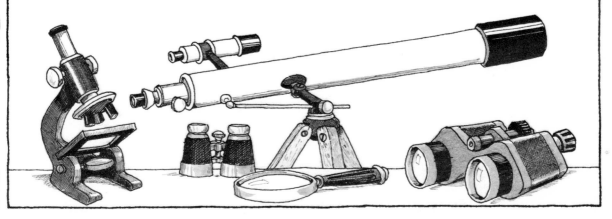

Look at a magnifying glass. Do you see the curve of the glass? This curve makes it a lens. Look through the magnifying glass at this page. Move the lens back and forth until the print is clear. Are the letters larger?

You can make your own lens in a very simple way. Put a small sheet of wax paper on the newsprint of a newspaper. Put a drop of water on the wax paper. Is the drop of water curved?

Look through the water and lift the paper slightly.

Do you see the letters? What happens to them as you lift the wax paper?

William Harvey (1578–1657)

William Harvey was an English doctor who studied medicine in Italy. One of his teachers was Galileo.

Harvey read many books about how blood moved in the body and he did many experiments on animals. He was the first scientist to do such experiments. For over 100 years before Harvey was born, doctors believed that blood in the body moved back and forth from the heart, but they did not know how this happened. Finally in 1616, Harvey discovered how blood really moves through the body. He found out that the heart pumps the blood through tubes called *arteries* and that the blood flows back to the heart through other tubes called *veins*. This is called the circulation of the blood. Harvey said that the heart beats or pumps about seventy-two times a minute in the human body.

Many years later an Italian doctor, Marcello Malpighi (1628–1694) discovered that arteries and veins in the body are connected by tiny blood vessels which he named *capillaries*.

William Harvey is often called the "father" of today's practice of medicine because of his important discovery of blood circulation.

Harvey's discovery of the circulation of the blood through the body has helped medical scientists learn how the different parts of the body work. It has also helped them to discover how to prevent and treat many illnesses and how to keep all living things healthier and living longer.

Press the fingertips of one hand to the underside of your wrist below the thumb of your other hand. Do you feel the beat? Count the number of beats you feel in one minute on your watch. We say you are "taking your pulse." You are really counting the beats of your heart as it pumps the blood through your arteries to all parts of your body.
See if you can take your pulse by pressing on other parts of your body. The picture shows you where these "pressure points" are.

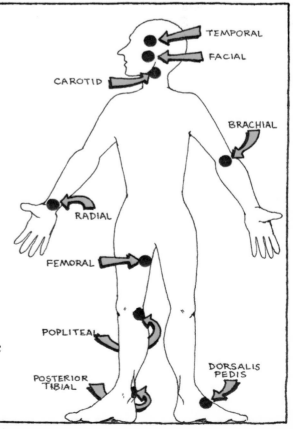

TEMPORAL

FACIAL

CAROTID

BRACHIAL

RADIAL

FEMORAL

POPLITEAL

POSTERIOR TIBIAL

DORSALIS PEDIS

Isaac Newton (1642–1727)

It was about 300 years ago, in England, that Isaac Newton was wondering what kept the Moon in space. One day, the story goes, as he was resting under an apple tree, he saw an apple fall to the ground. He thought that if the Earth's gravity could reach up into the air and pull the apple toward the ground, then gravity could also reach way out into space and pull the Moon toward Earth. "Why not?" he asked. Newton said that each heavenly body pulls the others toward itself. This is called *gravitational pull.* But, the Moon did not fall to the Earth.

The Moon is much smaller than the Earth. It is 240,000 miles (384,000 kilometers) away. The Earth's gravitational pull on the Moon is stronger than the Moon's upon the Earth. Why doesn't the Earth pull the Moon into itself? Newton said that the Moon is in motion and would keep moving away from the Earth but—the strong pull of the Earth keeps the Moon from flying off into space. This constant pull upon the Moon keeps the Moon moving around the Earth in orbit. So—Newton's laws explain that gravitational pull and motion, together, keep the moon in its orbit.

Isaac Newton was also a fine mathematician. He did many science experiments. He made a great scientific discovery when he experimented with a prism and found out that sunlight is really a combination of different colors—red, orange, yellow, green, blue and violet—the colors of the rainbow.

Our scientists use Newton's Laws of Gravitation to explain
the movements of the planets and their moons in the Solar
System. They have measured the different sizes of these
heavenly bodies and their distances from the Sun. Mercury,
the closest, is 36 million miles (58 million kilometers) away;
Pluto, the farthest, is nearly 4 billion miles (about 7½ billion
kilometers) away. Our Earth is 93 million miles (about 150
million kilometers) from the Sun. Scientists have figured out
how strong the planets' gravitational pulls are upon each other
and how fast they travel in their orbits around the Sun.
What scientists know about gravitation has helped them
send astronauts to land on the Moon and spaceships to land
on planet Mars, millions of miles from the Earth.

You can do something to help you understand how the Moon
stays in its own orbit around the Earth.
Put some marbles into a small cloth bag. Tie a long string to
the neck of the bag. Go outdoors into a large open lot where
there are no people around. Hold the free end of the string
and swing the bag around in a circle over your head. Think
of yourself as the "Earth," the string as the Earth's "gravity"
and the bag as the "Moon." The "Moon" remains in its orbit
as long as the "Earth's gravity" is pulling the "Moon." Stop
swinging. What happens to the bag? Why?
Now—swing the bag around again and then—let go of the
string! What happens this time? Why?

Benjamin Franklin (1706–1790)

As a young man in Philadelphia, Benjamin Franklin worked hard
and became a successful printer. He was always interested
in finding out how and why things happened around him. One of
his interests was electricity. At that time, about 250 years ago,
magicians used electricity to do tricks to entertain people.
After seeing one of these "shows," Franklin wanted to find
out more about electricity. He got electrical equipment from
England and did many experiments.
Franklin believed that lightning was really electricity.
One day during a rainstorm, he flew a silk kite high in the sky.
He had fastened a key near the end of the cord he was holding.
Franklin did not realize that this was a very dangerous thing
to do. Lightning struck the kite and traveled through the
wet cord, through the key, and sparks flew off the key.
Franklin discovered from this kite experiment that he could
make a lightning rod for his house that could carry lightning
down the rod and into the ground without striking the house
and causing a fire. From this time on, electricity was a
part of *science* and not of magic.
Benjamin Franklin is called the first American scientist.

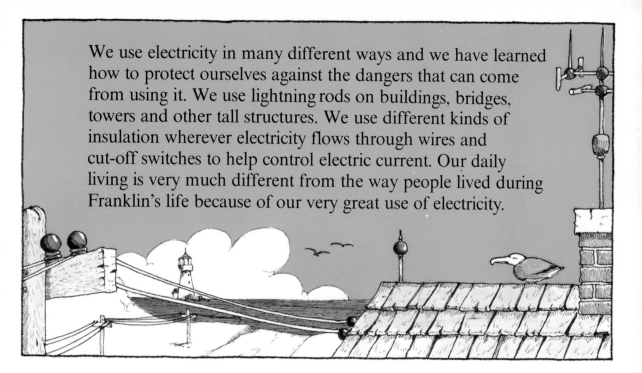

We use electricity in many different ways and we have learned how to protect ourselves against the dangers that can come from using it. We use lightning rods on buildings, bridges, towers and other tall structures. We use different kinds of insulation wherever electricity flows through wires and cut-off switches to help control electric current. Our daily living is very much different from the way people lived during Franklin's life because of our very great use of electricity.

After you come indoors on a cool day, take off your sweater. Do you hear a crackling sound? This sound is made by the sweater rubbing against you. We say that this rubbing makes static electricity, which jumps between you and the sweater and makes the crackling sound.
You can make static electricity another way. Drag your feet along the carpet and touch a metal doorknob.
Do you hear the crackling? Do you feel the tingle?

Scientists say that all things have tiny, tiny bits of electricity in them called electrons, and when things rub against each other, these electrons make static electricity. Lightning is a huge spark of static electricity jumping through the air.

James Watt (1736–1819)

James Watt was born in Scotland about 250 years ago. He
became an engineer and built bridges and canals, and also
worked at the University of Glasgow as an instrument maker.
Thirty years before Watt was born another Scotsman, Thomas
Newcomen, invented an engine that was run by steam and cold water
to pump water out of coal mines. The steam pushed the pistons in the
engine one way and the cold water pushed them back. However,
this engine did its work slowly and wastefully. Watt was
twenty-nine years old when he was asked to repair one of these
engines that had broken down. He saw how poorly the engine
worked. He believed that he could make it work faster and
with more power by using only steam to drive the pistons back
and forth in the engine. He built an engine to do this.
In this way, he really invented the *modern steam engine*, which
gave people a very powerful force to work for them.

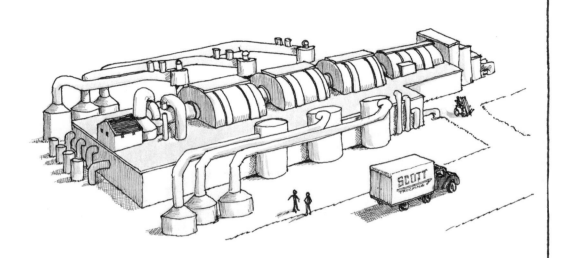

We have made many improvements over Watt's simple steam engine. We use these modern steam engines to drive huge machines in some factories. We also use steam to drive large turbines to make electricity. We even use atomic energy to make steam, which, too, can be used to make electricity. Scientists have honored James Watt by calling the unit of measure of electrical power—the *watt*. Our bright light bulbs use a higher number of watts than our less bright bulbs do.

You can see that steam can make things move. Half-fill a pot with water. Cover the pot with a loose cover. Boil the water on the stove. As the water boils, it makes steam. Does the cover jiggle? What really makes this happen? Everything is made up of tiny, tiny bits called *molecules* that move around. As the water gets hotter and hotter, the water molecules begin to rush around faster and faster. So—when the water boils, the molecules move so fast that some molecules fly out of the boiling water as steam molecules. They push!
The cover moves!

Joseph Henry (1797–1878)

In 1820, Hans Christian Oersted, a Danish scientist, found out
that when an electric current flows through a coil of wire,
the wire becomes a magnet. This magnet could pick up
very small things that had iron in them.

Five years later William Sturgeon, an English scientist,
heard about Oersted's discovery. He improved the Oersted
magnet by wrapping a copper wire eighteen times around a bar
of varnished iron bent into the shape of a horseshoe. When he sent
an electric current through this wire, the magnet was stronger.
It was able to lift iron up to a weight of nine pounds (four
kilograms). Sturgeon named his magnet—*electromagnet.*

Four years later, in 1829, Joseph Henry, a science teacher
in a New York State high school, improved Sturgeon's electromagnet. He covered some wire with silk and found out that
the more he coiled the covered (insulated) wire around the
bar, the stronger the magnet became. Finally, Joseph Henry
made an electromagnet so strong that it could lift a ton
(907 kilograms) of iron.

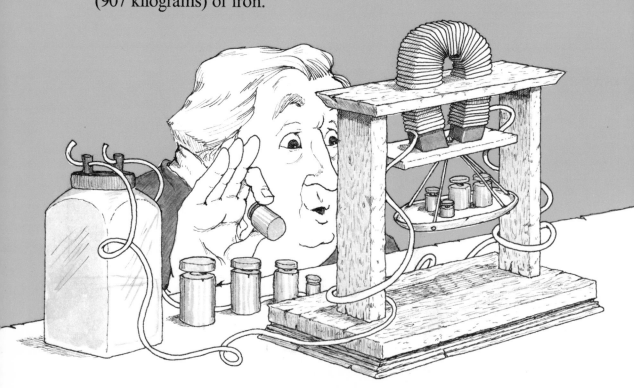

So you see—Oersted discovered something important, and Sturgeon,
Henry and others, using this discovery, improved upon it.

People who work in scrap-iron yards and steel factories use
huge electromagnets to lift tremendous weights of iron and
steel when they move these weights from place to place.
We use smaller electromagnets in electric motors, in bells,
in telephone and telegraph equipment to help make them work.

You can make your own electromagnet.
You can use a dry cell battery
and a long piece of covered bell wire.
You will also need a large iron nail and some small carpet tacks.
Take off about one inch of the covering at each end of the
wire. Coil the wire in one direction only around the nail,
leaving a short piece of the wire uncoiled at each end.
Attach one end of the wire to one pole of the dry cell.
Touch the end of the nail to the tacks. Lift! Does the nail
pick up the tacks?
Now—attach the loose end of the wire to the other pole of
the dry cell and touch the nail end to the tacks again.
Does the nail lift the tacks this time? You have made your
own electromagnet.
Find out what other small things your electromagnet can pick
up. Do not leave the electromagnet connected when you are
not using it. It will wear out the dry cell.

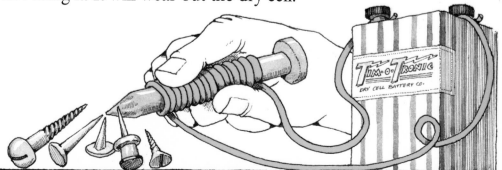

Louis Pasteur (1822–1895)

At the time Pasteur was born in France no one, anywhere, knew what caused many diseases. At the age of twenty-six Pasteur became a professor of chemistry in a French university, where he did many scientific experiments. As a result of these investigations, he found out that very tiny living things, called *microbes,* can make things change. He discovered that microbes turn wine sour. He soon found a way to stop this from happening. He heated the wine and then cooled it. This stopped the wine from turning sour and, in this way, he saved the French wine industry from failing.

These findings helped Pasteur discover that microbes, or *germs,* cause diseases in fowl, in cattle, in dogs and in people. He soon developed *vaccines* which he used to prevent diseases such as rabies. Sheep and cows were vaccinated against a disease called anthrax and poultry against another disease called chicken cholera.

Because of Pasteur's discovery that germs cause diseases,
our scientists have learned how to prevent and cure many,
many different kinds of diseases.
We drink milk that has been made safe by a process of heating
and cooling, called *pasteurization,* in honor of Pasteur.
Doctors and dentists use instruments that have been cleaned
of germs, or *sterilized,* with boiling water. We eat canned
foods that have been sterilized in factories by heating.
Scientists say that Pasteur's discoveries have done more
to prevent and cure diseases than the discoveries of any
other scientist.

You can show how microbes can make things change.
Add a teaspoon of dry yeast to some molasses and water
and mix well. After one day, you see the molasses solution bubbling.
These are bubbles of carbon dioxide gas. Smell the solution.
It smells like alcohol. If you have a microscope, look at a drop
of the solution through it. You will see many yeast cells growing
or budding. When this happens, a change is taking place.
We call this change—*fermentation.* Yeast cells change the
sugar in the molasses to alcohol and carbon dioxide.

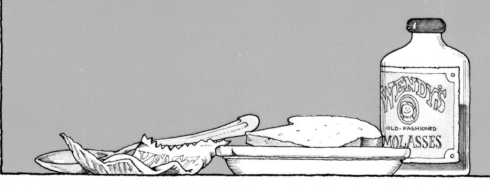

Thomas Alva Edison (1847–1931)

Thomas Edison knew that when electricity travels through a wire, the wire gets hot. He used this knowledge to help him invent the electric light bulb. Before doing this, he experimented with thousands of different kinds of thread materials collected from all over the world. He wanted to find the *one* thread that would get hot, so hot that it would glow and last for a long time, without burning up or melting. Finally, he discovered that a cotton thread coated with carbon could be used inside a glass bulb from which the air was removed. When he passed electricity through this thread, or filament, it became white hot and glowed for a long time without burning up or melting. In this way, Edison made the first successful electric light bulb.

Thomas Edison was born in Ohio and lived for eighty-four years. During his lifetime, he made over 1,100 inventions. Some of his best-known ones were the "talking machine," or phonograph, the moving-picture machine, a new telephone mouthpiece so that people did not have to shout into the telephone, a complete lighting system to light up a city, the mimeograph machine and even waxed wrapping paper.

People all over the world use electric light bulbs, but the filaments in these bulbs are now made from a metal called *tungsten* because tungsten glows brightly and lasts even longer than anything Edison used.

We also use other light bulbs without filaments. Some of these bulbs contain a gas called *neon,* which glows when electricity is passed through it.

Use a magnifying glass and look through the glass of a flashlight bulb. Do you see the thin wire? It looks like a coiled spring. This is the *filament.* Now—switch on the flashlight. Does the filament glow? When the electricity from the batteries in the flashlight flows through the filament it gets hot—so hot that it glows and we have light. Do you have a table lamp that has a clear glass bulb? Look at the filament in the bulb. Turn on the light. What makes the filament glow? What do you think happens when a bulb wears out?

George Washington Carver (1864–1943)

George Carver, whose parents were slaves, was born in Missouri
in 1864. After slavery was abolished, his former owner, knowing
that Carver was a fast learner who loved plants, sent him to
school. In high school Carver decided he would become a plant
scientist. At the age of twenty-seven he entered an agricultural
college where he studied how to prevent and cure plant diseases.
Soon after graduation, he was asked to become the first director
of agricultural studies at Tuskegee Institute. He stayed there
as a teacher and as a research scientist for the rest of his
long life. He found ways to make the soil richer, ways to grow
healthier plants and ways to turn many of these plants into
useful products. His greatest success came through his experiments
with the peanut plant. He discovered how to use peanuts to make
over 300 products such as oil, face powder, shampoo, printer's
ink, vinegar, milk, cheese, cream and buttermilk, dyes, soap and
even coffee. He also found out how to make starch, tapioca,
mucilage, artificial rubber and many other products from sweet
potatoes. He even discovered how to make paper, rugs and other
useful things from cotton.

George Washington Carver's fame spread all around the world.
He received many medals from the United States government and
also from several foreign governments.

Because of Carver's discoveries of the use of peanuts in so many different ways, peanut farming has grown tremendously to supply all the peanuts required.

There are many factories that make artificial rubber for tires, peanut oil for household use and many, many more such highly useful products.

George Washington Carver's plant discoveries have helped improve the life of people everywhere.

Shell a few peanuts and put them in a small brown paper bag. Crush the peanuts in the bag by rolling them with an empty bottle or a rolling pin. Do you see the spot on the paper bag? It was made by the oil in the crushed peanuts. Label this Spot No. 1.

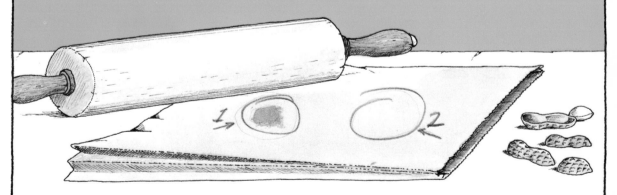

Put a few drops of water on another part of the bag. Label this Spot No. 2. Leave the bag on the table for two hours. Now—look at the bag. Which spot is still there? Why?

Robert Hutchings Goddard (1882–1945)

As a 17-year-old boy in Massachusetts, where he was born in 1882,
Robert Goddard dreamed about sending a rocket to the Moon.
After graduation from college, he became a professor of science
at a large university. In 1926, after years of experimenting,
he finally found out how to shoot off a rocket using liquid
fuel. He was the first scientist to do this. This rocket was
4 feet (1-1/5 meters) high and 6 inches (about 15 centimeters)
across. It burned gasoline with liquid oxygen as its fuel.
When this fuel burned, it formed hot gases that blew out of the
back of the rocket very rapidly. This made the rocket shoot
off in the opposite direction. It flew a distance of 184 feet
(about 56 meters) into the air. It traveled at the rate of
60 miles (a little over 96 kilometers) an hour.

Goddard soon made rockets that flew about 550 miles (885 kilometers)
an hour and to a height of 1½ miles (2-2/5 kilometers).
For many years, however, people did not really appreciate the
important work that Goddard did in rocketry.

Using Goddard's ideas, scientists have built huge rockets of several sections. They use these powerful rockets to launch spaceships that carry men and equipment far off to the Moon. When these space vehicles travel fast enough to escape from the gravitational pull of the Earth, they then coast through space on the way to the Moon. Scientists have even sent off spaceships containing special instruments that have landed on the planet Mars, many, many millions of miles away. Some of these instruments do important experiments and radio back the information to the scientists on Earth. Today we finally recognize that Goddard is really the "father of modern rocketry."

Tie one end of a long, thin cord to the back of a chair and put the other end of the cord through a drinking straw. Tie this end to the back of another chair. Pull the chairs apart until the string is straight across. Blow up a balloon and hold the neck tightly. Stand behind one of the chairs. Ask your friend to fasten the blown-up balloon to the straw with pieces of scotch tape, keeping the neck of the balloon toward you. Now—take your fingers off the balloon. Watch the balloon shoot off toward the other chair as the straw helps keep it moving straight across. Why does this happen? When the air pushes out of the balloon toward you, it sets up a push in the opposite direction and the balloon shoots off away from you.
Does this help you understand how rockets and jet planes work?

All over the world, there have always been people who were interested in finding out why and how things happen. There were also those who wanted to find out how to do things better and more easily. These people were our scientists and inventors. In this book you read about only a handful of the many, many thousands of these very talented people, but—these few, in their wonderful work, did so much to change the way we think and act in our daily living.

There are more scientists and inventors alive and working today than have ever lived all through history—trying to find new cures for diseases, looking for more information about the heavenly bodies, seeking to discover new sources of fuel for energy, experimenting to find still newer ways of making and using things of all different kinds.

Do you think that you would now like to find out about other scientists? Do you think that, someday, you would like to become one among the world's famous scientists and inventors?